"Phil helped my business partner and me get our business on track again. He was our counselor, our confidant, and our miracle worker — compassionate, caring, and one hell of a golfer!"

Kimberly J. Anderson
Attorney, Anderson and Boback

"I had a client struggling with creating a culture of accountability, initiative and results amongst all level of supervisors. Everyone wanted to deflect to "management" when things did not go right and who were very resistant to change. Phil came in, assessed the situation and crafted a program that helped the supervisors understand the nature of leadership and why it was important to them personally and the success of the organization. Thanks to Phil's guidance, easy to understand and implement programs, supervisors are now empowered to answer employee questions, solve problems and actually make suggestions for possible improvements in operations, among other areas. The change has resulted in improved employee relations and efforts, the redirection of company resources to productivity and away from having to solve morale and productivity problems that had no need to exist. Everyone is much happier and the company results reflect a better environment overall."

Andrew S. Goldberg
Partner, Laner Muchin, Ltd.

"This book is like talking directly to Phil. Each chapter tees up valuable lessons. Some old, some new - altogether insightful. Highly recommended!"

Naveed Usman
Principal & CEO, Usman Group

"Phil has the insight and vision to help business owners and professionals become better leaders. I have been privileged to work with Phil and greatly value his opinions, thoughts and advice. He creates an environment where business leaders can effectively collaborate, communicate and empower one another. Simply put, Phil makes organizations better."

Elliot Richardson
President & Co-Founder
Small Business Advocacy Council

"For the first 11 years of my legal career I thought of bringing in my own clients like hitting a hole in one; something that a few other people could do, but out of reach for me. Phil helped to show me my own blind spots and how I could create my own opportunities by setting my own visions. After going through the coaching sessions, I feel like I can write the next chapter of my career, instead of having it written for me by someone else.

Going through Gafka's business development program was awkward for me at first, since the vocabulary and golf analogies were new to me. But it was, in many ways, like going from black and white into color, because there was so much more right in front of me than I had realized. The benefits were not only finally generating my own revenue, but also a much more positive view of my own work and co-workers. I still don't play golf, but I've had tangible results from Phil's coaching that have transformed how I look at my practice."

Matthew Stevens
Stone & Johnson, Chartered

"Thanks for starting us on a leadership journey, and helping us to communicate effectively with each other. Your coaching and insight made all the difference."

Susan A. Oldenburg, CPA, EA
Oldenburg Accountants & Advisors

"Phil saw something in me, he believed in me from our first lunch together and from then on, became my business coach. If you are looking for someone to give you the answers, perhaps Phil isn't your guy. While I'm not a golfer and know barely anything about the game, Phil boosted my confidence in a way that propelled me to take action and held me accountable along the way.

What I loved about working with Phil is that it was always MY agenda and not his. He had a way of always bringing it back to me. And those are the things that helped to propel my business in ways I'm truly excited about today. Phil has high standards and expects you to work - to follow through on the tasks you say you will. But, he's also very reasonable and understands when a shift needs to be made or something has to get put aside. He's a personable guy who cares about your family as much as he does your business."

Rebecca Gruenspan MSW
RG Adoption Consulting

"Phil is an Ace of a person and has tremendously helped me with my leadership skills by speaking in a language I can understand. By connecting a sport I love, golf, to leadership, my communication and leadership skills have improved as I lead my two businesses and serve on two non-profit boards. Phil is a great man helping others to be greater!"

John Gotschall, CLU
Coaching Financial

"When help was needed to determine where I wanted my business to go and how I was going to get there, I knew the only way to get to these answers was Phil. Phil provided the guidance necessary by helping me face the tough questions that when answered lead me in the right direction. Phil stands for (gentle) Prodding, Helpful, Insight, Lasting (results) and I am forever grateful for such an exemplary professional coach!"

Janice L. Boback
Anderson & Boback

"For over 30 years now Phil has been the single biggest reason for my success. He has the vision, ability, and experience to identify, confront, and address issues faced by leaders. The analogies of these challenges and issues to golf are spot on. I highly recommend spending the time to read this refreshing view of leadership skills. Fore!"

Dennis Skrypchak
Senior Vice President
Morgan Stanley

"Early on, in life, you choose to lead or follow. It's mostly a quiet choice based on instinct. Leading, then, increases your daily distance from following. Phil positively helps you impact the lives of those around you. You're better for it and so are they. What a marvelous blessing!"

Paul Heinze
Goldberg Heinze Business Advisors

Hole-in-One Leadership
9 Proven Steps Guaranteed to Get You Extraordinary Results

(The Front Nine)

Philip Gafka, CBC

First Edition Design Publishing
Sarasota, Florida USA

Hole-in-One Leadership,
9 Proven Steps Guaranteed to Get You Extraordinary Results
The Front Nine
Copyright ©2019 Philip Gafka

ISBN 978-1506-908-04-5 PBK
ISBN 978-1506-908-05-2 EBK

LCCN 2019937853

April 2018

Published and Distributed by
First Edition Design Publishing, Inc.
P.O. Box 17646, Sarasota, FL 34276-3217
www.firsteditiondesignpublishing.com

ALL RIGHTS RESERVED. No part of this book publication may be reproduced, stored in a retrieval system, or transmitted in any form or by any means — electronic, mechanical, photo-copy, recording, or any other — except brief quotation in reviews, without the prior permission of the author or publisher.

This book is dedicated to the wonderfully smart and strong women I have known, Mom, Nani, Deborah, Marissa, Ani and Janet.

Writing this book has been a journey for me and there are many people to thank – Sarah Victory, Carol Keene, Lauren Kelliher, Brian Swanlund, Dennis Skrypchak, Ron Cerrudo.

I'd like to thank my Beta readers: Randy Popp, Nirag Patel, Naveed Usman, Dr. Chris Wigfield, Connor Greenlees, Richie Marrero and Bill Burnett.

Table of Contents

Foreword 7

Introduction 9

Hole #1 Vision
Make It Big and Own It 13

Hole #2 Culture
Identifying How to Do What You Do 21

Hole #3 Culture
Living Your Honor System 27

Hole #4 What's In Your Bag?
Skills and Abilities 33

Hole #5 Playing Your Game
Leadership vs. Management 39

Hole #6 Hazards
What Hazards? 45

Hole #7 Practice, Practice, Practice
More Practice 51

Hole #8 The Art of the Recovery Shot
Getting Back In the Game 57

Hole #9 Drive for Show, Putt for Dough
What the Pros Know 63

In the Clubhouse 67

Glossary of Golf Terms 70

Foreword

Phil Gafka has hit the nail on the head with his comparison of leadership to the game of golf. There is nothing more important than managing your attitude in golf, just as if you were running a business. It is not about every decision being the right one, but learning from each situation to be better equipped when a similar problem arises.

With this book, you will not only gain a better understanding of what it means to be a leader, but also how to improve and grow in the role. By providing real life experiences and quotes from professional golfers, the reader will see a unique point of view relating to the subject.

As a former PGA Tour winner and PGA Professional who has given more than 35,000 lessons, I can confidently say that you never stop learning. This applies to both the technical and mental aspects of the game – many of which can be applied in everyday life. This book has given me a new insight on how to better myself as a teacher and a man. If you are looking to improve your leadership qualities both personally and professionally, I highly recommend reading *Hole-in-One Leadership*.

Ron Cerrudo
PGA Professional
Director of Instruction,
The Daniel Island Club

Introduction

Why would anyone link golf with leadership? To me, they are the perfect parallel. Both are more of an art than a science. They require development by the honing of specific skills. Each is a dynamic process and subsequently, a thing of beauty when expertly accomplished. Golf and leadership are my most passionate lifelong pursuits.

My leadership journey has run parallel to my self-discovery through the game of golf. To fulfill a graduation requirement, I signed up for a golf class my last semester of college. It was spring. What could it hurt? Within two months of graduating I started my first job. I quickly realized that golf was an integral part of the business environment I had joined.

My leadership journey includes a 30+ year career in Corporate America, working up from sales to management to leadership. During those years I had the opportunity to work with and observe many companies and I realized the differences between well-run, successful enterprises and organizations that continually struggle.

These common denominators that exist, or were absent, are the basic tenets of this book and the foundation for the executive and leadership coaching I have been doing since 2008.

My clients are in a diverse range of industries and sectors – manufacturing, distribution, retail, non-profit, health-care, and professional business services. This wide variety of clients all need help clarifying where they are going and how they are going to get there. And how to lead.

I was first exposed to leadership in high school. I was elected to the student council, then went on to serve as the sophomore class president. I found both experiences to be humbling. There was a lot more to leadership than I imagined. The more I learned, the more I wanted to learn and the more there was to know. Knowledge and experience are what make leaders and golfers rise from average to great.

Golf, like leadership is an individual challenge—it's you, the club and the ball. In leadership, it's you and the next challenge.

What is hole-in-one leadership? The reference to hole-in-one is the single best shot in golf. All golfers aspire to it. Teeing up a ball on a par three, we share a version of the same thought, *this one is going in.* Swing. Watch the ball hit the green, track toward the hole and drop in. At that moment everything you've learned, practiced and studied comes together. Voilà, a hole-in-one. I'm fortunate to have made a heart-stopping hole-in-one.

The company I was working for hosted a dealer training trip/factory tour (read four days of golf) in Arizona. It would have been hard to create a better scenario than playing a round of golf with our company's three biggest customers.

We engaged in a typical *friendly* match with plenty of competitive talk and a few dollars riding on the outcome.

We were on the 17th tee of a par three hole, a mere 148 yards to the green. I was the last golfer to hit. One of my opponents claimed my shot would not matter, as he was going to sink his relatively short putt for a birdie (one under par). My partner countered that he was going to chip-in his ball that was just off the green, for his birdie. I teed up my ball, executed my unique golf waggle and took a swing at the ball.

Following the flight of my shot, my first realization was that the direction was looking pretty good, as my shot appeared to be fairly well aimed. Tracking the ball as it continued its flight, it was clear the trajectory was headed in the vicinity of the hole. The remaining question was how accurate was the distance of my shot?

The awareness that my shot was going close to the hole suffered a momentary setback when the ball disappeared. Then we all heard the clang of the ball hitting the flagstick as it entered the cup. Voilà, *my* hole-in-one.

The leadership parallel lies in every opportunity, challenge and situation. On the golf course, the hole-in-one doesn't happen every time. In business, you won't always make the perfect leadership decision. But knowing that you're equipped with the skills to accomplish it, you will go forward to be a hole-in-one leader.

You don't have to be anyone but yourself. With the help of the information presented here, you'll gain a better understanding of your true self and the skills and traits that make you who you are, where you want to go and how to get there. You'll be able to take advantage of the gifts that you already own to achieve your results. Whether you play once or twice a year or have never played a round of golf in your life, you will be able to relate to the tips in this book for improving your personal and professional leadership ability.

The *course layout*, or how this book is laid out, consists of nine *holes* or chapters, the front nine. Each chapter is dedicated to a key leadership element, paired with a quote by a professional golfer relating to the chapter's content. You'll encounter some golf terms, which you may or may not know, so I've included a *Glossary* of golf terms at the end of this book.

We'll cover the importance of knowing which clubs are in your leadership bag, how and when to use them. You'll craft a vision for yourself and your organization. And clarify the merits of leadership vs. management.

Supporting the content are sections labeled:

> **Fore!**—detailing actual client stories, demonstrating how/where/when clients wound up in the rough or facing a tough leadership challenge.

> **Back in Play** is how coaching helped my clients to reframe their thoughts and actions to lead them to their desired results.

These stories illustrate how applying leadership skills drove their organizations to improved results, their collective holes-in-one.

You will find two holes devoted to Culture, because it is *that* important.

At the end of each hole are two sections. One is called:

Gimmes (a short final putt conceded in casual play) the takeaways from what you've just read.

The other is the **Driving Range**. It's your practice time. I heartily encourage you to participate and invest time on the *Driving Range* exercises. Some will be easy, and some will be quite challenging. It might be the first time you've had to come up with leadership answers for yourself.

Stay with it, work hard, be honest, and unlock the potential that lies within. Turn that potential into the personal performance that will produce results — your personal or professional hole-in-one.

Hole #1

Vision
Make It Big and Own It

"One of the most fascinating things about golf is how it reflects the cycle of life. No matter what you shoot — the next day you have to go back to the first tee and begin all over again and make yourself into something."
Peter Jacobsen

In leadership and golf, you must decide what game you're playing. Your chosen game will determine the trajectory of your career, and more importantly, your impact on your leadership journey. How you play — within self-limiting confines of attitudes and habits or stretching to grow your talents, skills, abilities and results — should be your best vision of you. The path we take determines our destination. What path are you on? Have you given it much thought? Whether a personal path or the one on which you are leading your organization, knowing where you want to go matters.

Individuals, teams and companies are ever-evolving. Next month or next year, you will end up somewhere else. Where that will be depends on the path you take. Let's take a moment to clarify the terms *vision* and *mission*, because they are different.

Vision is the big goal — why we do what we do, and how we will measure our success. Visions include being an innovator or leader in your industry or solving a problem that betters humanity. Some visions might appear to be unreachable, but you're on your way to achieving yours and giving it everything you have.

Missions are smaller, bite-size chunks of the vision. Missions have a place in your journey. They are more immediate challenges to be overcome on your way to achieving your vision.

If you are planning on playing one of your best rounds of golf, your initial mission would be to play Hole #1 successfully, scoring a par or possibly a birdie. The mission changes – play Hole#2 successfully, again par or a birdie. And so on. Eighteen successful missions on the way the a great round of golf equals your vision.

One would guess all pro golfers have the vision of achieving the Grand Slam. The Grand Slam is winning all four major championships — the Masters, the U.S. Open, The Open and the PGA Championship — preferably in the same year. Golf professionals would settle for accomplishing this during the course of their careers. To do it in one year is a *big* vision. Bobby Jones is the only person to have accomplished a Grand Slam in one year, in 1930. There are only five golfers who have achieved a Career Grand Slam: Gene Sarazen, Ben Hogan, Gary Player, Jack Nicklaus and Tiger Woods. Imagine a vision so *large* that a mere half dozen professionals claim the honor.

If winning the Grand Slam is the vision, then the first mission is to win the first major tournament of the year, the Masters. Next, win the PGA Championship. Then the U.S. Open and then The Open.

The vision never wavers. For the pros, it's the Grand Slam. For you, it's the vision you're aspiring to. The missions change as you accomplish them and overcome those challenges. The vision stays intact. You should achieve your missions within a six to eighteen-month span.

Your vision needs to be concise. Convey it like a mantra in one meaningful statement. In crafting a vision, make it yours. Make it big. Once you're thinking big, think bigger. Then bigger still — your personal Grand Slam.

Once you have honed your vision, own it. Commit to all strategizing, planning, organizing and actions (everything) in pursuit of achieving your vision.

When your vision is for your organization, your next step is to communicate it effectively to each and every person in your organization. This communication goes beyond just knowing they hear you or it. They need to understand it. This communication needs to be at a personal level because *they* need to own the vision with you. We are looking at the big picture — 10, 20 years forward.

Your vision might be so big that you might not be the one to achieve it. However, you'll travel in the right direction, setting goals, accomplishing your missions and moving ever closer to accomplishing your vision. Owning your vision is the pivotal difference in individuals who achieve great success, versus those who settle for par for the course.

Your vision becomes the guiding light for all strategies, tactics and actions, and these components need to be in alignment. That's owning your vision. We often hear the phrase *getting our people working together*.

When I'm playing golf, some days my drives are exceptional — long, straight and in the fairway. But there are times I can't hit an accurate shot from the fairway to the green, to save my soul. Or it's vice versa. There are days when my driving game is solid, as well as my fairway or approach shots, but I can't buy a putt. Then there are days, the hole looks as large as a manhole cover, and I make most of my putts, but it has taken me one or two extra shots to get to the green.

It's a very successful day on the golf course when all aspects of my game, are working together and my score is low. It's the same feeling when everyone in your organization is working together to achieve the improved results you've been aiming for. That's alignment and ownership of your vision.

When all the pieces and parts of your organization are working together, toward this type of synergy, imagine what you can accomplish.

Visions should be big, and you can see from the examples to follow, there's nothing small about what these companies are working toward.

> *"To bring inspiration and innovation to every athlete in the world."*
> **NIKE**

> *"To make people happy."*[1]
> **DISNEY**

> *"To provide access to the world's information in one click."*
> **GOOGLE**

Fore!

A conversation with a frustrated client:
Carl: "My people don't get it."
Me: "What is it that your people don't get?"
Carl: "Where I'm trying to go."
Me: "Where are you trying to go?"

Carl explained a vision for his decorative stone manufacturing company. In the next breath he said "or..." The moment he said "or," it was easy to identify the problem.

I knew Carl to be an extremely creative person. His ideas sprayed forth like golf balls at a driving range. Being that creative, he produced a vision du jour.

---

[1] A recent Wall Street Journal article reported that Disney was facing challenges of cleaning up the illegally scattered cremains of deceased fans who wished to have Disney Properties as their final resting place, because it was their *happy place*. Talk about accomplishing your vision.

My response to Carl was, "Someone in your organization isn't getting 'it,' but respectfully, it isn't your people. It's you."

Carl's company was successful but not without a consistent array of roadblocks. And by his "or" reference to his vision, many of those challenges were self-induced. Chasing shiny objects was a standard in Carl's nature, part of which made him successful and part of which caused his business to encounter more bumps in the road than necessary.

Back in Play

My challenge was to help Carl crystallize his vision and commit to it. We discussed the growth direction and aspirations for his company for the next ten years. After working at it for a period of time, as it rarely comes in one sitting, Carl was able to create and articulate his vision.

The next step was to get his people to understand and buy in. He did that by calling a meeting to explain the vision, as Carl now knew where he wanted to go. The key to this meeting was to not just tell them the vision, but to discuss it and let them become a part of the ownership of the vision, insuring their buy in. And with their input, the vision actually grew.

He was able to lead his people forward, achieving the objectives, goals and missions in pursuit of their vision. No more stops and starts, spinning in circles or running in place.

The results of their clear vision were impressive. Within four years, his company doubled their annual revenue.

Your vision must answer questions that arise, such as when someone asks, "Should we be doing this?" You should be able to answer with your own question, "Does it support our vision and where we're going?" Leading your employees to their own answer helps them support the vision. If the action supports the vision, do it. If it doesn't, don't.

Make life simple for you and your people. Teams respond to clear direction and clear purpose. A clear vision becomes your default for direction, policies, processes, goals, etc. Your vision must be real, it must be yours, and, of course, BIG.

Fore!

I asked a new client whether or not she had a vision. Ashley said, "Sure, I have a vision." When asked to stand up and tell it to me, Ashley obliged. It wasn't the most compelling vision, so I asked her to continue standing. My next request was for her to restate her vision, but this time to proclaim it like she really meant it. There was some improvement. "Please," I told Ashley, "state it like you own it." Ashley responded, "I can't." She couldn't because it wasn't her true vision. Giving lip service to a vision that you cannot stand up and say it like you own it is a recipe for unfulfilled goals, confusion and dissatisfaction.

Ashley was working hard. Her days were filled with activities, meetings and deadlines. She just wasn't getting the results she wanted. Working hard and being busy doesn't always translate into success when you're unsure of where you're headed.

Back in Play

Through a series of meetings and many questions, Ashley crafted a vision that she could stand up and say it like she owned it, because she did. It was truly hers. It was not nebulous or vague. It came from deep within her, a vision that sincerely motivated her and the people that were on her journey with her. Ashley grew her business, bought another business and tripled revenue in two years.

Being able to own your vision makes all the difference. It should be clear, concise, big and yours. Clarity is essential to communication. One client created a vision statement that included the term *maximize resources*. What does a phrase like *maximize resources* mean to every department and each level of staff? The executive leadership team may understand, but everybody should know what that means to them in their jobs. When the vision is understood by everyone, its effect is profound. As a hole-in-one leader, it is up to you to continually drive home the vision by using examples to reinforce the vision you're trying to achieve.

Gimmes

- You need to have a clear vision for where you're leading yourself and your organization.
- It must be a vision you *own,* anything less won't cut it.
- You must communicate it clearly at every level.

Driving Range

- Create your vision — one for you and one for your organization. Be able to stand up and say it like you own it — because you do. And because you do, the people who hear it will understand it and can help you on your journey to achieve it.
- Think BIG. Limit your statement to one sentence with no *run-on* sentences. (Make your grammar school English teacher proud.

Notes:

Hole #2

Culture
Identifying How to Do What You Do

"Success in golf depends less on strength of body than on strength of mind and character."
Arnold Palmer

Enterprising leaders operate their businesses with a greater understanding of their culture: more open and honest communication, greater candor, higher levels of integrity, and more fun and results. It's not only getting people to agree on how they will communicate, but also getting them to be accountable to the agreed-upon core values.

Peter Drucker, famous management consultant, is credited with the saying, "Culture eats strategy for breakfast." You might have the ideal vision for you or your organization, but without the proper culture to support your vision, the odds are stacked against you.

When individuals or organizations commit to how they're going to conduct their business, moving forward takes total commitment and accountability to core values. Be clear about what's right and wrong, acceptable and not, and to what you will hold yourselves and each other accountable.

Fore!

While working with David, on developing his IT company's culture, he and his team defined honesty as a major core value. During our discussion on core values, a team member came in with an urgent client situation. The employee whispered to David that a customer was on the phone and wanted to talk immediately. David audibly whispered back, "Tell him I'm not in."

Upon hearing the exchange, we called an official timeout to discuss this situation and its implications. David had asked a person not to be honest. We examined how well that aligned with their core value of honesty.

Back in Play

This proved to be a great learning opportunity to help the organization understand core values are not just words on the wall, but words to commit to and run their business by. As a result of some lively discussion, they changed this particular core value from honesty to integrity, because they felt they could practice integrity better than they could live with brutal honesty.

We zeroed in on the integrity discussion and asked what it meant to each individual in the room. The agreement was that integrity is where you draw the line in the sand; the line you don't cross. The challenge was to agree on that line.

The group came together with an understanding of how they were going to define and live with integrity, across the board, without exception. In other words, what talk they were going to walk.

The current United States Golf Association *Rules of Golf* is 205 pages, including 26 index pages by which you can quickly reference every situation. I'm not recommending anything near that level of complexity for you or your organization, but you do need to define your rules, it's your culture. Don't think in terms of penalties. Think of positively moving yourself forward. Forward motion becomes easier when you understand the penalties for not holding yourself and your people accountable to your core values. Have candid conversations when team members don't live up to the company values. It's an important part of building and maintaining your culture.

Fore!

A client, Justin, asked me for help when his business was consistently falling short of their sales targets. As we talked about his firm, he was perplexed because everything seemed right, yet they were not attaining their sales goals. He was swift to respond when I questioned him about the culture of his financial services firm.

"It's simple," he said. "Be nice and show up on time."

"That's it? Would you pay me to do that?" He cocked his head and looked at me, trying to figure out if I was joking or not.

"I'm serious," I continued. "If that's all it takes to work here, then I'm on board, but is it enough?"

Justin hadn't ever defined his company's culture. His superficial statement had no real direction and lacked parameters to help guide his employees to how they were going to conduct themselves in the day-to-day running of their business.

Back in Play

In meeting with Justin's leadership team, we explored what they wanted their culture to be. We identified the attitudes and behaviors that were needed and desired. We also identified the behaviors and characteristics that would not be tolerated.

Their newly defined culture focused on a hand full of things, including achieving results, in addition to showing up and being nice.

By changing their culture and committing to getting the results they knew they could achieve, they proceeded to attain their sales goals for each quarter and the total year.

Once culture is defined and applied, trust within the organization begins to blossom and grow. With a shared culture, your people think and act together, with an understanding of how they are going to create desired results and move ever closer to achieving your company's vision.

On this level of employee ownership of the organization's culture, you collectively have a much better shot at achieving your vision. Strive to be consistent with your culture, both internally with your people and externally with your customers. The key to remember is that behavior, yours and your peoples', is really what defines your culture. It isn't just a description written on a poster. Your behavior is what matters most, because your team will follow what you do and what you allow others to do.

Gimmes

- Your vision will not be accomplished without the proper culture to support it.
- Defining your culture is not enough, you must commit, own it and live it.

Driving Range

- Identify your culture. Keep it to a handful of core values expressed as words, bullet points or a short sentence. Like your vision, these core values must be big – big enough to guide your organization forward.

Notes:

Hole #3

Culture
Living Your Honor System

*"If you win through bad sportsmanship,
that's no real victory."*
Babe Didrikson Zaharias

Culture is where golf and leadership run parallel. Other sports such as basketball, football, hockey, soccer and tennis use a referee, linesman or umpire, who call fouls, penalties and infractions. Not so in golf. Not so in your leadership role.

Golf is a game where you assess penalties on yourself. It's called the Honor System. You know the rules and how the game is to be played. As it is with your leadership role. In the previous chapter you defined your own culture to guide you and your organization. As hard as it seems to define your core values and set your culture, it can be tougher to live it and hold yourself accountable.

The core values you choose define the culture you are committing to. You create your own rules for your leadership journey. Since you've made them, you know when you've crossed the line and dishonored the culture you've cultivated. Call yourself out for those violations. Moving forward, hold yourself accountable to your culture and don't violate it. Own it.

Fore!

My client Walt was recommended for coaching because he was deemed "disruptive" by the organization. The offending descriptors were: disrespectful, talking down to people, didn't encourage or build up team members, didn't listen, just ordered people about.

Walt was a surgeon conducting serious, complex and life-saving surgeries. Walt admitted the disruptive descriptors listed above were accurate, but in turn he didn't feel he was getting the best from his team. In his own defense of his negative behaviors, Walt stated he was not getting the best team members the hospital had to offer. The reality was, in emergency surgery you get whomever is on call. You get what you get.

Walt's blind spot was that regardless of the on-call surgical team, he was the leader and it was his responsibility to lead the team to insure successful results.

Back in Play

Walt had been managing negatively and needed to learn how to lead positively. The key was to get Walt to understand the culture in the operating room was set by example, his example. He had control but was managing instead of leading.

I spent time coaching Walt to help him realize he was the driving force of the culture in the operating room. Until then his culture had been negative. What he needed to own was a positive culture in order to get the positive results he wanted, saving lives.

We defined what a successful and positive atmosphere really looked like at the high-velocity time of emergency surgery. Walt committed to it, owned it and executed on his culture. He was willing to call himself out if he stepped back into disruptive behaviors.

Walt changed his leadership style and atmosphere in the operating room improved dramatically. Not only did Walt become aware of his influence on the team, he also learned that he could lead improved results from everyone on the team, regardless of who happened to be on-call.

Owning your culture is holding yourself accountable to what you've committed to. Because if you do that, you also have the right to hold your people accountable to the same standards.

Think about yourself and the people in your organization. How well would you say you're owning your culture? Are you just talking the talk, or are you walking it as well? When committed to your culture you can hold one another accountable. You and others must be willing to make the hard decisions regarding yourself and fellow team members, in order to live within your honor system.

Fore!

XYZ Manufacturing, a commercial building products company, was facing a decline in sales as well as declining morale inside the company. They were addressing the two major problems. Through our discovery discussions my interviews with a cross section of people in the organization exposed the reason for the decline in morale — a culture of tolerating bad behavior.

XYZ challenged themselves to come up with a culture that would support their people and their company's growth.

The leadership team arm-wrestled over core values, how they defined those terms and identified the behaviors that supported their new culture. They drew lines they agreed they would not cross. They were aligned and committed. Employee "town hall" meetings explained to everyone in the organization how the culture was changing and encouraged all team members to embrace the new culture.

XYZ's leadership team faced a major hurdle. They handled a few of the easier cultural challenges, now came the first hard one. Their top sales person, Bill, didn't adopt the new core values and the associated behaviors.

Bill said he was on board, but he violated the values with his usual poor behavior. Since his lack of change was apparent to everyone else, it was addressed in three separate meetings, with him, by the leadership team. Each time Bill said the right things and agreed to change, but the change never happened.

XYZ was faced with a simple question — to tolerate Bill's unacceptable behavior or let him go?

Back in Play

Any organization can step up when it's easy, it's what they do when faced with a tough situation. If they're true to their culture there's really no other answer than to do what's right — act on their words and commitments.

After the third meeting with Bill, the promised changes still hadn't taken place. The leadership team fired Bill, living up to their honor system. It's very hard to fire your top sales producer, but Bill's position as top sales person was not as important as having everyone in the organization aligned. The rest of the sales team divided Bill's accounts and grew their sales even higher. The leadership team's decision to fire Bill was difficult, but the effect on the rest of the organization was incredible.

The leadership team truly understood XYZ was more than just talking the talk. They were willing to walk it as well. The commitment to their new culture was real. By leading with the bold action of letting their top sales person go, the organization united in a way they had never done, and sales grew dramatically.

That's the interesting thing about culture. Your people will listen to what you say, and they're going to watch what you do. If your actions align with your words, you own your culture, and your people will join you. If all you do is talk, they'll see right through it and know this new culture initiative is just talk. Leaders learn that culture is not what you say, it's what you tolerate.

Culture is the most crucial component to get right. After defining your core values and committing to live by them, you now have the culture you want and can own it. You own it by honoring what you've committed to.

Gimmes

- You need to define and own your culture.
- Do the right things in alignment with your values.
- When the referee, linesman or umpire goes away and their function is replaced by the work of you and your people, that's when you are truly living by the *honor system*.

Driving Range

- What action do you need to take, right now, to live within your honor system? What's next?

Notes:

Hole #4

What's In Your Bag?
Skills and Abilities

"Rhythm and timing are two things which we all must have, but no one knows how to teach either."
Bobby Jones

Having the right tools and knowing how to use them is essential to playing your best game, on the course and in the office.

If ever attending a professional golf tournament, pay attention at the driving range and around the putting green to see what equipment the pros are packing. No two hit with the same woods, irons, wedges or especially, the same putters. Seasoned professionals have spent years honing their game and their equipment, customized to their exact specifications.

Likewise, check your golfing buddy's bag the next time you're on the links. Odds are you're not playing with the same selection of clubs.

No two golfers use the same equipment, just as no two people lead in the same manner. We are all different, and our leadership styles are as unique as we are.

When facilitating leadership seminars, I ask participants who they look up to as great leaders. I get showered with names of business, political, religious and military leaders, along with mothers, fathers, friends and bosses.

Next, I ask *why* they are viewed as leaders. What admirable leadership traits and characteristics do these people exhibit? The responses are as numerous and varied as the leaders chosen — great communicator, commanding presence, visionary, patient, good teacher, mentor, orator, motivational, focused, strategist and more.

Leadership, like golf, requires a highly individualized set of skills, experience, knowledge, values and motivation. Just as no two golfers wield the exact same equipment, how they *use* the *clubs in their bags* is the leadership difference. Success requires using your distinctive skills and applying them to the best of your ability.

Fore!

Elizabeth owned a family services business that was not doing well. She was overly concerned with how her competitors ran their businesses, instead of being focused on her business. We explored why she was in the family services arena to begin with. The rocky situation she had endured throughout her own childhood instilled in her a passionate desire to help others.

Back in Play

Elizabeth was clear about why she started her business, but the years had clouded her view of what her basic motivation truly was. Once that spark was reignited she was able to focus on her "why" and not the activities of her competitors.

When Elizabeth reunited with her true motivation, it no longer mattered what her competitors were doing. Her clients were better able to identify with her. To no surprise, her business increased dramatically. What mattered was her "why" — her motivation. Talk about a "go-to" club.

In the game of golf, you may carry a maximum of 14 clubs. Each leader, as well, has a distinct *set of clubs*, with tools and techniques that make her a uniquely effective leader.

You probably have a few go-to clubs you can confidently rely on, and in which you have a great degree of confidence. In your leadership role, you might have a few go-to skills you count on. But, are you using all the clubs in your bag?

Behavioral psychologists have found that the more intense or stressful the situation, the more people react in a conditioned manner. In the heat of the moment we default to that conditioned response. But a leader should *act* not just react.

Becoming a better leader is about making use of the full complement of all your skills and abilities, not just the ones used as a reflex. The goal is to use all the clubs in your bag. Leadership development is about using and improving the tools and techniques that define great leadership for you. You continuously learn which clubs to use and when.

A recurring theme with my clients is helping them to recognize their leadership tools and how to implement additional techniques to get their desired results. Powerful leadership takes more than just expanding current strengths. The greater challenge is improving weaknesses. That is how to become a more well-rounded leader.

I've had the good fortune to witness many great leaders in action. Some have been the most unlikely leaders you could imagine. What impressed me most was every great leader I've met was not trying to be someone else. They were the best versions of themselves. Some people are referred to as *born leaders*. I think leadership skills are *developed*.

From the following list of leadership descriptors, which are you born with and which do you develop? — compassionate, motivational, visionary, effective communicator, humble, decisive, focused, driven, honest, forthright, hardworking. Clearly, these traits can be developed, so anyone can grow into a better leader.

It's hard to view oneself objectively, which is why I use assessment tools with my clients. We get an overview of their *how, what and why* — establishing a baseline to focus on what matters most.

You can spend time and attention improving any skill. When I see a leader on stage employing great presentation skills, motivating the workforce or team, it's doubtful that person was as effective and smooth the first time upon taking center stage. Understanding skills as continually developing and improving is another step toward becoming a hole-in-one leader.

Get to know all your clubs and wield them with confidence to become the best version of you. There is no limit to how many leadership skills you can develop and put into practice.

Are you viewing your leadership growth as a journey? Because that's exactly what it is. No one can be great at *everything;* no one is expected to be. Being a great leader will require the best version of you. This is *your* game. Take it to the next level.

Fore!

Nick had started a software/data analytics company based on software he wrote. As the company grew, he was drawn deeper into the day-to-day running of the company. The administrative duties consumed an increasing amount of his time and attention, negatively effecting his role as the top salesperson. Consequently, there was a dip in sales and growth.

Back in Play

Through our discussions Nick realized he was the best sales representative for his company because he had the most in-depth knowledge of the software they were selling. Nick hired a Vice President of Operations to handle the day-to-day running of the company. He refocused his energy and efforts on sales and returned to growing top-line revenue.

Nick, like other leaders, was capable of performing many of the roles within his company. Deciding which were the most important roles (choice of clubs) at any given time is an ongoing challenge.

Gimmes

- Your leadership style is yours and yours alone. Get comfortable with it and own it.
- Recognize the immense number of clubs you get to put in your leadership bag. There is no limit.

Driving Range

- List an honest assessment of your leadership skills, traits and characteristics. Write all of them down — the good and the bad.
- Decide which skills, traits, characteristics are your core strengths, your go-to's, which you will continue to reinforce. Which ones need further development?
- If you are uncertain of your true strengths and weaknesses, talk to someone you trust, who has worked with you or for you, and ask for their honest input. You'll surprised at their responses.

Notes:

Hole #5

Playing Your Game
Leadership vs. Management

"Golf is the loneliest sport. You're completely alone with every conceivable opportunity to defeat yourself. Golf brings out your assets and liabilities as a person. The longer you play, the more certain you are that a man's performance is the outward manifestation of who, in his heart, he really thinks he is."
Hale Irwin

Leadership, like the game of golf, is about understanding what you truly have to work with and then using it to the best of your ability. In Hole #4 you inventoried the leadership clubs in your bag. Next is how you use those clubs, the leadership skills and abilities you own.

Let's first clarify leadership versus management. Peter Drucker once explained, "Management is doing things right, and leadership is doing the right things."

A focus on leadership doesn't mean there isn't a place for management, but I find most people spend far too much time managing and not nearly enough effort leading. In the system of American business, employers start elevating people into managerial positions. Along with moving up the corporate ladder, people are trained to think and act like managers. In other words, we get what we ask for.

Oftentimes businesses do an inadequate job of training their people to manage, so things normally go downhill from there.

The other common situation, which most of us have been exposed to, is working for a micromanager: someone who hovers and tries to make sure that you and everyone else does everything in exactly the same way — *doing it my way or the highway.*

Leadership is different, starting with doing the right things. That's abiding by the culture established by you or your organization. Those right things include communicating, inspiring and motivating your people. Teach them not only *how* things need to be done, but more importantly, how to figure out for themselves how to accomplish *what* they have committed to do.

That's another key difference between leadership and management. Management is *how* to do things right. Leadership is about establishing *what* needs to be done and growing your people, so they can figure out the *how* for themselves. Guiding them to grow is more about leadership than you think.

To get the best and most out of your team, you must be a good leader. Urging them to think, make decisions, allowing them to make non-fatal mistakes and, most importantly, stay out of their way until they need you.

Management diminishes the responsibility of employees to think on their own. Most of the time they are waiting for the next directive, the next *how* to do something.

Managing enables team members to pass all the thinking and decision-making back to the manager. Wouldn't you prefer to get the best out of everyone on your team by tapping into all of them — especially their minds?

The tough part of this challenge is letting go of the *old school* thinking of top-down management, in which decisions and directives are fed down the chain of command, so *managers* can hold onto their authority — the right to give orders.

Leaders are not concerned with who is credited, they are attracted to achieving the desired results. If the team accomplishes those results, everyone wins. As the leader, that is exactly what you're trying to achieve.

Fore!

George was the owner of a multi-location retail operation. He started the business and grew it over the course of twenty years. One day when I entered his office, he was price-checking a large number of vendor invoices. Upon inquiring how long it had taken him, he responded with usually 4-6 hours per week.

George explained that with tight margins, controlling costs was paramount.

We agreed that controlling costs was very important, but I questioned further why he was performing that task. Despite it being an important function in managing his business, double-checking pricing could be handled by someone else in the organization at a more effective pay scale. If that employee found a discrepancy, they could surely bring it to George's attention.

This is a classic example of a leader not doing the right things. In this case, George was spending 16-24 hours per month checking vendor invoices. It was not the best or most productive use of his time. The larger issue was George could have used those hours leading and growing his company. There was a "lost opportunity cost" for the leadership role in those hours devoted to the price-checking process.

Back in Play

George desired to become a better leader —he delegated the review process to someone else in the company. He also recognized other managerial duties he was performing that could be easily taken off his plate.

That example of learning how and why to delegate created a shift in the way George's business was run. Each member of his leadership team was tasked with delegating three responsibilities that could and should have been done by a more appropriate team member.

This shift in thinking and action led to all members of his leadership team investing more time in leading instead of managing. This resulted in his company's achieving its largest increase in sales and profit in seven years.

Fore!

Katie was lamenting about it being the end of the year and time for employee evaluations. No one in her real estate franchise liked the process. Managers didn't like filling out review forms, and employees did not receive much value from the review meetings. Everyone felt it was not time well spent, and the results were hard to quantify.

Our discussion was well timed, as we were identifying the culture changes Katie wanted to make. Clearer communication was high on the list of cultural values needing improvement. Why were they waiting months to try to correct something or praise someone that had done well?

Back in Play

We explored a better way to do both — better communications and better employee feedback could be combined into daily conversations and interactions. Katie and her team started giving immediate feedback when it would have the greatest influence or impact, instead of annually.

Employee response was overwhelmingly positive. They heard what they were doing well and where they needed to improve, on a timely basis. Productivity increased along with profits, as Katie's company began to clarify and implement this integral component of its culture.

Annual reviews now serve a new purpose. They focus on big-picture discussions, reinforcing organizational alignment, vision and culture. They also create personal growth and development goals for each employee.

Gimmes

- Leadership and management are different.
- Delegating management duties creates time for leadership.

Driving Range

- Assess the *managerial* activities that you are doing, and delegate them to someone appropriate.
- List leadership activities you can now work on in the time you've opened up by delegating.
- Evaluate the timing and effectiveness of the feedback you're giving your people.

Notes:

Hole #6

Hazards What Hazards?

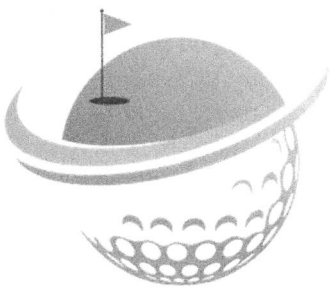

"Of all the hazards, fear is the worst."
Sam Snead

Expect hazards. Know they are there, but do not fear them. Fearing a bad shot increases the odds of making one. Knowing there is a sand trap up ahead in the fairway allows you to strategize how to play around it. Golf courses provide little pictures of the hole layout on the scorecard. Therefore, most hazards on the golf course can be anticipated. Better courses now have a GPS to show where all the hazards are and your distance from them. Even with all that knowledge, golfers still find a way to get into the hazards.

In developing your leadership skills, there are many known pitfalls. Despite foresight, you'll still find yourself in a few. Some are subtle, others are obvious. There isn't a GPS or hole-by-hole card pointing out what leadership problems lie ahead.

One of the challenges in golf is strikingly similar to one in leadership: it's not just about avoiding the hazards, but knowing how to get out once you're in them.

Hazards become less daunting when we are prepared to deal with them. No matter how well we play our game of golf or how well we hone our leadership skills, we *will* encounter hazards. Don't beat yourself up about it. The answer is to learn how to deal with them. Do you let hazards defeat you, or do you persevere?

Golf's strategic thinking aspect is course management: assessing the course and analyzing its overall degree of difficulty. Depending upon personal skill level, a golfer might choose to play tough courses a bit more conservatively.

Course management in leadership is learning how to best play the next challenge you face. Those challenges have a risk-reward relationship. Leaders have to take their next shot calculating the best *overall* results. Sometimes it makes sense to try for the riskier shot, while understanding every risk has a downside. The only path is forward, so it's *how* you play.

Fore!

Emily was a risk taker, which many times had a negative effect on the growth and progress of her family-owned chain of upscale car dealerships. Emily saw risk as something to be confronted, not feared. The missing component was the realistic assessment of what could go wrong, and how it would negatively affect the business, due to her decisions. She had a blind spot regarding risk.

Back in Play

By tracking a series of risky financial decisions, we were able to put a dollar amount to the losses her company had incurred. This shed a light on the overall negative impact it had on her company's future. Emily needed to reframe what was to be an acceptable risk level. She set financial boundaries to guide her decision-making moving forward.

After two years, her company was once again thriving. She still takes risks but is disciplined in her approach.

Another of the hazards in leadership is not bringing your "A-game" — your absolute best every day. In order to grow, you also need to stretch. Go a step faster than the day before. Increasing pace and building endurance allows you to sprint at the critical moments.

It's not about sprinting the whole day. It's about working at your pace, knowing when to sprint and having the stamina to do it. You need to play your A-game *every day*.

Fore!

It was a particularly trying time for Bob's custom home building company. During one of our meetings Bob grumbled he felt as if he were climbing a mountain every day.

I asked, "Who put the mountain there?" Bob came to realize that he put it there. He had a negative attitude about his pace of life; everything had become an uphill battle and he wasn't playing up to his leadership potential.

Back in Play

We talked through a positive change of attitude regarding his leadership when Bob realized he was holding himself back. We came up with new imagery, including a vista of the third hole at his favorite golf course— long and flat. It helped Bob see he only had to put one foot in front of the other, making it easier to bring his A-game every day. This new visual changed his attitude about the day-to-day challenges of his business.

Fore!

Judy's county government office was undertaking a massive cultural shift from "the way we've always done it" to implementing productivity standards in a government workplace.

Her department was sabotaging its transition with daily road blocks comprising of "what if" questions. Her staff didn't want to be held accountable for productivity standards until they had answers to every question they could think of.

Judy was managing the daily bombardment of "what if" questions by delaying the implementation of productivity standards. Her people were leading better than she was.

Back in Play

Judy was sharp, coachable and quick to grasp onto her leadership role. Her recovery shot out of this hazard was to overcome her fear, make the conscious decision to lead this change and not try to manage it.

Judy stepped up her A-game, set a date for establishing the productivity standards and instituted a policy of answering questions and issues as they actually arose.

Gimmes

- Count on hazards along the way. They are just part of the game.
- Playing your A-game every day will help you deal with the hazards.

Driving Range

- Create a list of Strengths, Weaknesses, Opportunities, Threats (SWOT Analysis) for yourself and your organization. Weaknesses and threats will be your potential hazards. Being aware of these hazards will help you avoid them and recover when you find yourself in one.

Notes:

Hole #7

Practice, Practice, Practice
More Practice

"Most players practice until they get it right. Great players practice until they can't get it wrong."
Annika Sorenstam

Practice makes for improved results. It is the same for leadership and golf. It's a never-ending journey. Like your golf swings, not all your leadership moves are going to be great ones. Mistakes and bad habits picked up along the way reinforce what practice is all about.

Leading isn't about being perfect. It's about being as excellent as possible. The more you practice, the more you hone your skills, and the closer you'll actually come to achieving your vision.

The Wednesday before a golf tournament is the most interesting: the practice round. Watching the pros dissect the course, specifically the greens, is a study in the ultimate importance of practice.

The pros spend 15 to 20 minutes getting a feel for each green, anticipating where their potential pin placements will be. They know the hole locations will be changed each day of the tournament. They actually hit shots to different sections of the green, from the front and back, left and right, to learn that green and its nuances. When match time arrives, and the cup has been placed, golfers can execute their skills to the best of their abilities, because they have practiced and they are well prepared.

Golfers are not only gifted athletes with tremendous touch and feel, but they are also working professionals and understand the value of practice.

My first real taste of the game of golf was in my senior year of college. New to the game, I was, as expected, atrocious compared to seasoned players. My then-girlfriend's father invited me to play at his country club with him, the country club champion, and a PGA professional named Ron Cerrudo rounded out our foursome. At best, I should have been caddying that day and not playing.

Ron executed wonderful shot after shot. I marveled at each one and did a fair bit of hero worshiping. At one point Ron faced a shot that forced him to go either right or left around a tree. He asked me to choose, and again, he executed a beautiful shot.

The bigger story of the day was the club champion's opportunity to play against and hopefully beat a touring PGA professional. Club Champ was trying his hardest, and Ron was doing his best to prevent him.

On the 18th hole, Ron was in a green-side sand trap. He settled over his ball and hit a flawless sand shot that landed softly and rolled into the hole for a birdie. At this point the club champion's dream of victory had truly gone up in smoke. He had been beaten by the PGA pro. He was obviously upset and made a comment to the effect of "you couldn't do that again..."

They stood close to one another, exchanged a few words and made a bet. I didn't hear their quiet conversation and had no idea what the stakes were. Ron flipped another ball into the same sand trap. He stepped in and executed another wonderful shot that put the ball in the hole again. At that point my hero worship turned into adoration.

Over conversation at the 19th hole, Ron told me, "I practice eight hours a day, five days a week. If I let a club champ beat me, I should give up my PGA card."

The concept of practice wasn't new to me, but Ron drove home the point. Ron, a PGA tour professional, demonstrated the *value* of practice.

When reading about great golfers, you learn how critically important practice is to the success of their game. Pros go out to the driving range after their round to work on a *single shot* that failed that day. They hit that shot over and over and over until they know they can count on it the next day.

The value of practice is to improve your game. In any competitive environment, your competition is practicing their game as well. To win the next round, or the next business deal, you must bring your A-game.

The time you are willing to invest in practicing your leadership skills will have a direct influence on the outcome and the results of your leadership journey. It has been said anything worth doing is worth doing well. Are you committing the time and attention to practicing your appropriate leadership skills?

Fore!

After designing and manufacturing women's accessories for more than five years, Joan's company had grown, but not as consistently as she had at the beginning.

We explored what she was doing when things were going well and what was different when sales began to decline.

Even though Joan had practiced what it took to start and initially grow her business, consistent growth became illusive. It begged the question — what needs to be done to make growth more consistent and sustainable?

Back in Play

We identified the activities that Joan was practicing during the growth cycles of her business. We also identified what she wasn't doing at the time when sales declined. What Joan came to realize was she wasn't always practicing the meaningful activities that contributed to her sales growth. Just as sales hit a good level, Joan would stop doing some of the foundational activities that were known to elevate her business to successful levels.

We created a list of activities including daily, weekly, monthly practices Joan needed to practice to insure consistent growth.

Joan grew her business, not only consistently, but to larger increases than she had previously accomplished.

If you don't want success to be a series of peaks and valleys, you must practice the foundational activities that got you there on a daily basis.

Practice is important, as it helps you improve your technique so you can hit great shot after great shot. Practice also supports your leadership role, completing your goals, your missions and getting ever closer to achieving your vision.

Fore!

I used to have a knack for hitting out of a sand trap. Then I lost it. For the life of me I could not hit a ball out of the sand. During a practice session, if I threw 20 balls in the sand and took 20 swings, I'd have 20 balls still left in the sand. I was practicing, but on the wrong things. For all my hours in the sand, I couldn't see what I was doing wrong.

One frustrating morning before an afternoon tee time, I called the local golf course and asked if there was a teaching pro available for a lesson — immediately.

Back in Play

At the course Sandy (appropriately named) threw some golf balls in the sand trap and told me to take a couple of swings. In under a minute she said, "I see a few adjustments you need to make." With that, I had my old skill back.

Point being, I couldn't see what I couldn't see. We sometimes need an unbiased third party to give skillful guidance.

Gimmes

- Practice is important, no matter your level of expertise.
- Practicing the right things, the right way, is more important than just practicing.

Driving Range

- List the leadership skills you've mastered.
- Identify what you practiced to get to that level.
- Identify the leadership skills you want to improve and begin practicing them in the same manner.
- If this is a big challenge it might be time for a coach.

Notes:

Hole #8

The Art of the Recovery Shot
Getting Back In the Game

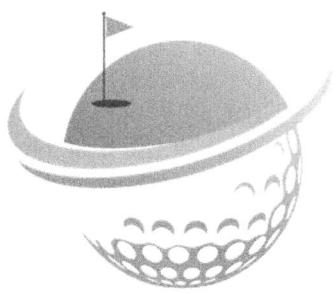

"One minute you're bleeding. The next minute you're hemorrhaging. The next minute you're painting the Mona Lisa."
Mac O'Grady

Consider all the variables you encounter in your golf game and leadership quest. Now imagine the challenges and mistakes you'll face along the way. It's up to you to anticipate them and come up with a strategy.

Knowing how to get back in the game is the magic behind the recovery shot. It's part of being a strong player and leader. Think art, not science. Science is in the details of *what* needs to be accomplished. Art is the graceful, fluid manner in which you *accomplish* it. A specific recovery shot might not be something you can practice, but it is something you can prepare for.

The recovery shot is about crafting different ways to use the tools at your disposal. It forces you to think and execute at a different level.

There are two keys to mastering the recovery shot. *Creativity* is the ability to alter your swing to make a particular shot or seeing a unique solution to solve a new business challenge. *Confidence* comes from experience, getting out of the rough or tough situation, because you've done it before.

Your tee shot feels okay when you hit it, but it begins to fade, moving to the right. Coupled with a nasty bounce, it winds up snuggled up against the base of a tree. You might be able to get a clubface on the ball, but your backswing is impeded by overhanging branches. The only direction to advance the ball is sideways.

How often have you encountered a similar challenge, either on the course or in business? How often have you practiced that exact shot on the driving range? Probably not too often.

Given the choice, we tend to practice normal shots under driving range conditions: no trees, roots or low hanging branches. This is where to practice the science of your swing: the basics, mechanics and execution. With the confidence of that knowledge, you can alter your swing to hit your successful recovery shot.

Up against the base of a tree, or facing your next unexpected leadership challenge, start thinking in terms of *art* — creating and executing new solutions. Consider the possibilities, options and adjustments. Then muster the confidence to take the shot.

As technology and the internet change the way business is done, past solutions might not make the cut for current problems.

Doing the same things over and over and expecting a new result is Einstein's Theory of Insanity. If that describes you, then it's time to do things differently. Is this next shot merely to get out of trouble and set up the next shot? Or is there an opportunity, with creativity, to actually advance the ball or your business?

Fore!

John was a partner in a commercial building products company that expanded into the newly acquired building next door where he located his office. We were working on changing the culture of their company to more open and honest communication and a more positive work environment.

John and his six partners were in charge of leading the cultural change and things were not going well. During our conversations, John appeared to accept his 1/7 share of the responsibility, even though he had tucked himself away in an annex, out of the everyday workings of the company. By lack of proximity, he was unable to add his influence on the cultural changes.

I posed the question, "Are you doing enough or just your share?"

Back in Play

John knew he had the respect of the employees and realized he could leverage it to do his share. Not an equal share, his share.

John's recovery shot was to move his office to the main building, connecting to and interacting with more teammates. One small physical move became one strong cultural statement to the entire company. John's willingness to move and accept a larger leadership role directly influenced the cultural change. Communication, attitude and productivity showed a marked improvement within two weeks.

Sometimes the best recovery shots happen when you limit your options instead of expanding them. The smallest adjustment can yield a huge variety of results.

One day you might find your business in a bit of trouble. The competition didn't do what you were expecting. What is *your* recovery shot?

You have two choices. Play safely within your game or elevate yourself to the next level. It comes down to your creativity and your confidence.

Fore!

I was part of a group meeting with Tom, a CEO, and his twelve directors of a large senior living facility. They had an authority issue. Things were not being decided on and action was not being taken. I asked the group who felt they had the authority to properly do their job. Three of the 12 raised their hands. One woman started to raise hers and then withdrew it.

Tom called a break and I followed Tom to his office. Tom said, "I'm at a loss. If I was clear on anything, it was that my people knew their level of authority, especially Beverly."

Back in Play

When the authority issue presented itself, Tom began to understand that there was a disconnect. What was clear in Tom's head did not match what was in the minds of his directors. To resolve the issue, they had to come to an agreed-upon definition of authority.

Tom and his directors aired their concerns and discovered although they were given responsibilities, Tom had not given them the proper authority to act on those responsibilities.

They defined their responsibilities and Tom delegated away the requisite authority, then got out of the way to let his people do their jobs.

The organization ran faster and more efficiently than ever before, as everyone was more powerful and effective.

Have you been in a situation where you felt totally at a loss? You thought you knew the landscape only to find out you didn't know the real lay of the land.

When faced with a challenge, don't shrink back. Step up and tackle it with creativity and confidence. Learn from your mistakes and choose your best path forward from wherever you find yourself. Sometimes your need of a recovery shot isn't because of an error; it just is.

You will face times when there is no shot. You can't even swing at the ball. You have to *take a drop* — a measured distance from the hazard where the ball can be dropped, and the penalty stroke associated with it. The leadership equivalent of taking a drop might be in saying I made a mistake, I'm sorry, or I was wrong.

Gimmes

➢ Getting back in the game is the art of the recovery shot. Don't let an errant shot derail you.
➢ It is in the recovery that your genius is often revealed.

Driving Range

➢ The next time you face a challenge, look at it from a different perspective. Assess the problem, make a creative decision and then execute your best recovery shot — with confidence.

Notes:

Hole #9

Drive for Show, Putt for Dough
What the Pros Know

"You know what they say about big hitters... the woods are full of them."
Jimmy Demaret

You have to love the above quote because it's so true. Big drives are beautiful to watch — the arc of the shot, the truly amazing distance the ball carries. Long drives are impressive, especially if they end up in the fairway.

Drives are important. They are a part of your *long game*, or hitting the shot with a full swing. They're just like the work you've done along the way to set your vision and define your culture. It's an important part of the game. However, you have to hit again.

The approach shot, hopefully one that lands on the green, comes from using a variety of the clubs in your bag. It's similar to solving your next leadership challenge.

The *short game* is all those shots you're faced with to get to the green. It also includes the things you have to consider such as: distance, wind, uphill, downhill, trees and sand traps. They are the nuances that go into making a successful shot.

Your leadership short game is identifying and analyzing what or where you need to *lead* next. For instance, it could be coaching a team member to a clearer understanding of your culture or a better alignment of their efforts toward your vision.

Golf analysts talk about *putting for dough* on Sunday afternoon, the last day of a typical four-day tournament. Making the winning tough putts under a great deal of pressure, is putting for dough. Very much like the leadership game, it's getting to the end, completing the missions and achieving the vision.

When putting, the ball either falls into the hole or not. There's no gray area. It's the same with achieving results. If your vision, culture and communication are aligned, you achieve your goals.

Your leadership journey is about achieving results. Have you truly done all you can? You are the only one who can determine if you gave it your all and brought your A game. Your effort and attitude make the difference.

Fore!

Nancy is a partner in a law firm. In our early November coaching session, she asked me to help her formulate an excuse as to why she wasn't going to make her billable hours for the year. I respectfully declined.

Nancy was rather taken aback. I asked which she would rather be, a partner that came in six weeks in advance, having already decided to give up, or one who came in on December 31st and said, "I did everything I could, but fell short?"

Back in Play

Nancy committed to doing whatever was necessary. She focused, worked hard and made her billable hours for the year. She also received a substantial raise. She learned to always give it her best shot — her putt for dough.

Don't tell yourself it's over before it's over. Don't defeat your efforts with negative self-talk. Don't give up. As Winston Churchill said, "Never, never, never give up," and, "If you're going through hell, keep going." I'm not sure how good a golfer Churchill was, because he also said, "Golf is a game whose aim is to hit a very small ball into an ever-smaller hole, with weapons singularly ill-designed for the purpose."

The long drives might be beautiful to watch, but you also have to get the ball in the hole. That's where the money is.

Now that you know leadership fundamentals, you are ready to become a Hole-in-One-Leader.

Gimmes

- ➤ To achieve your vision, you need a long and a short game and everything in between.
- ➤ Get the ball in the hole, it's your putt for dough.

Driving Range

- ➤ Get in the game. Go tee it up and hit your own personal hole-in-one.

P.S. It's okay to hit more than one.
~ Phil Gafka

Notes:

In the Clubhouse

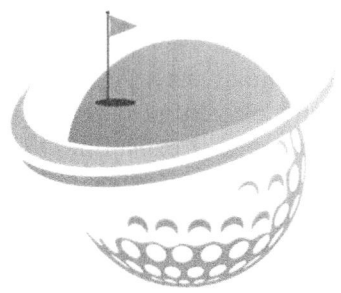

"Do your best, one shot at a time, and then move on."
Nancy Lopez

You picked up *Hole-in-One Leadership* for any number of reasons. Perhaps you like golf and thought, *what could it hurt to learn something along the way?* Maybe I signed a book for you at an event, or you were curious about how I linked my favorite pastime with my career. It's possible you actually wanted to improve your leadership skills. The nine chapters you've just read have cleared some of the obstacles from your leadership path.

So, what next? What will you do with your heightened understanding of yourself, your vision and your culture? With newfound awareness of the clubs in your bag, what will you do with them?

Take out your notepad and begin to practice at the *Driving Range*.

Are you ready to create a vision for you and your organization? You should be willing to stick your neck out and define a culture that's representative of you and your values. Do what the successful people around you are doing: hard work, homework and practice. Are you ready to get serious? Then it's time for practical application.

If you watched a tutorial on improving your golf swing, you'd pick up a club, perform a waggle, position your feet and swing. Leadership may not be *exactly* like that, but it can be viewed in a similar way. You are learning to tweak approaches new and old, along with understanding it's a mental game of finesse and execution. You're discovering challenges can be fun and rewarding. Improving your game becomes part of who you are. As a leader, you are always evolving.

In time your new leadership skills will become comfortable, familiar and an integral part of you. You will become resilient, confident and empowered. It is not your job to stand over people and micromanage. It *is* your role to lead the souls of people to want to join you on your journey. You have a job to do as a leader, and if you're a good one, you'll want to be even better.

Decide right here and now that you want to be a better leader. Be willing to change. Let go of managing and step into leadership. Changing your thinking can change your leadership results and, in turn, your life. Adopt the mindset of a Hole-in-One Leader, making every shot as good as it can be, while setting yourself up for the next one.

A hole-in-one is not going to happen every time, but you will think of it and try for it every time anyway. If that is your goal, you are going to shave off some strokes and improve your game. But it's impossible to make a hole-in-one if you don't play the game. You gotta be in the game to win.

So, are you ready to go to the driving range? Are you thinking, *I gotta call Phil*? Wonderful. I'm at the ready. You'll find me on the back nine.

Notes:

Glossary of Golf Terms

Ace: When a player hits the ball directly from the tee into the hole with one stroke. Also called a hole in one.

Approach shot: A shot intended to land the ball on the green.

Birdie: A hole played in one stroke under par.

Bogey: A hole played one stroke over par.

Bunker: A depression in bare ground that is usually covered with sand. Also called a sand trap. It is considered a hazard under the Rules of Golf.

Bunker, green-side: A bunker bordering a green.

Bunker, fairway: A bunker located on or in the fairway.

Chip: A short shot (typically played from very close to and around the green), that is intended to travel through the air over a very short distance and roll the remainder of the way to the hole.

Chip-in: A short shot, detailed above that goes into the hole, also called the cup.

Club: An instrument used by a player to hit a golf ball. A player is allowed to carry up to fourteen (14) clubs during a round of golf.

Club-face: The surface of the club-head which is designed to strike the golf ball. Striking the ball with the center of the clubface maximizes distance and accuracy.

Clubhouse: A building on a golf course providing facilities for golfers, typically including changing rooms, bar, restaurant, offices for club officials and noticeboards with information about local rules, the conditions of the course, upcoming events etc. A clubhouse may incorporate a pro shop and dormie house. The clubhouse is normally located adjacent to the first and final holes of the course.

Course: A designated area of land on which golf is played through a normal succession from hole #1 to the last hole.

Cup: Also referred to as the "hole."

Double bogey: A hole played two strokes over par.

Drive: The first shot of each hole, made from an area called the tee box (see definition below), usually done with a driver (a type of golf club).

Driver: Longest and most powerful of all golf clubs, with a large head and a long shaft for maximum club speed and distance.

Driving range: Designated area where golfers can hit practice golf shots.

Eagle: A hole played in two strokes under par.

Fade: A shot that, for a right-handed golfer, curves slightly to the right, and is often played intentionally by skilled golfers. An overdone fade will appear similar to a slice.

Fairway: The area of the course between the tee and the green that is well-maintained allowing a good lie for the ball.

Flag-stick: A tall marker, often a metal pole with a flag at the top, used to indicate the position of the hole on a green. Also called the pin. An additional smaller flag, or other marker, is sometimes positioned on the flag-stick to indicate the location of the hole (front, middle, or back) on the green.

Fore: A warning shout given when there is a chance that the ball may hit other players or spectators.

Gimme: Refers to a putt that the other players agree can count automatically without actually being played (under the tacit assumption that the putt would not have been missed). "Gimmes" are not allowed by the rules in stroke play, but they are often practiced in casual matches. However, in match play, either player may formally concede a stroke, a hole, or the entire match at any time, and this may not be refused or withdrawn. A player in match play will generally concede a tap-in or other short putt by his or her opponent.

Golf club: An implement used by a player to hit a golf ball. A player is allowed to carry up to fourteen (14) clubs during a round of golf. (ii) An organized group of golfers, usually owning or managing a golf course. (iii) The entirety of a golf facility, including course, club-house, pro-shop, practice areas etc.

Grand slam: Winning all the golf's major championships in the same calendar year. Before The Masters was founded, the national amateur championships of the U.S and the UK were considered majors along with the two national opens and only Bobby Jones has ever completed a grand slam with these. A "Career Grand Slam" is having won each of the majors at least once, not necessarily in the same year.

Green: The area of specially prepared grass around the hole, where putts are played.

Hazard: Any bunker or permanent water including any ground marked as part of that water hazard. Special rules apply when playing from a hazard.

Hole: A circular hole in the ground which is also called "the cup", 4.25 inches (108 mm) in diameter.

Hole in one: Hitting the ball from the tee into the hole, using only one stroke.

Iron: A club with a flat-faced solid metal head generally numbered from 1 to 9 indicating increasing loft.

Lie: How the ball is resting on the ground, which may add to the difficulty of the next stroke.

Links: A type of golf course, usually located on coastal sand dunes.

Long game: Shots that take place from the tee box or the fairway with the longer clubs in your bag, and a full swing.

Major(s): The most prestigious golf tournaments. In the modern game the Masters Tournament, U.S. Open, The Open Championship and the PGA Championship are considered the men's major golf championships. The Kraft Nabisco

Championship, LPGA Championship, U.S. Women's Open, Women's British Open and The Evian Championship are currently considered the women's major golf championships. Historically, from before the dominance of the professional game in the mid-20th century, the British and U.S. Amateur Championships are also often considered men's majors. Sometimes, people refer to The Players Championship as "The Fifth Major".

Mulligan: A do-over, or replay of the shot, without counting the shot as a stroke and without assessing any penalties that might apply. It is not allowed by the rules and not practiced in tournaments, but is common in casual rounds in some countries, especially the United States.

Out-of-bounds: The area designated as being outside the boundaries of the course. When a shot lands "O.B.", the player "loses stroke and distance", meaning that he/she must hit another shot from the original spot and is assessed a one-stroke penalty. Out-of-bounds areas are usually indicated by white posts. As an example, if a player's first shot from the tee comes to rest out of bounds, a one stroke penalty is assessed and the player then plays the third shot from the tee.

Par: Standard score for a hole (defined by its length) or a course (sum of all the holes' pars).

Pin: Slang for flag-stick.

Pre-shot routine: The steps an experienced player goes through to get ready for his or her shot. It usually involves taking practice swings and visualizing the intended shot.

Pro (professional): A golfer or person who plays or teaches golf for financial reward. They may work as a touring pro in professional competitions or as a teaching pro (Also called a club pro).

Putt: A shot played on the green, usually with a putter.

Rough: The grass that borders the fairway, usually taller and coarser than the fairway.

Short game: Shots that take place on or near the green. Putting, chipping, pitching, and green-side bunker play are all aspects of the short game.

Tap-in: Often called a "gimme", a tap-in is a ball that has come to rest very close to the hole, leaving only a very short putt to be played. Often, recreational golfers will "concede" tap-ins to each other to save time.

Teeing ground: The area from which you hit your drive or tee shot. The teeing ground for a particular set of tees is two club lengths in depth. The ball must be teed between the markers, called tees, that define the teeing ground's width, and no further back than its depth. Tees are colored, but there is no standard for colors. The "teeing ground" refers to one set of tees. Most courses have at least three sets of tees; some have more than twice that many. The areas where tee markers are placed are called "tee boxes".

Tempo: The smooth change of the speed of a player's swing from first movement, through the ball strike, to the follow-through.

Waggle: A pre-shot routine where a player adjusts his body, the club, and/or practice swings at the ball.

Wedge: A type of golf club; a subset of iron designed for short range strokes. Of all the categories of clubs, wedges have faces with the highest degrees of loft.

Glossary taken from Wikipedia

Made in the USA
Monee, IL
27 April 2026

49090742R00046